Endangered Wildlife

Jen Green

Published by © Atebol Cyfyngedig 2010

Published in 2010 by Atebol, Fagwyr Buildings, Llandre, Aberystwyth, Ceredigion SY24 5AQ
www.atebol.com

ISBN 978-1-907004-52-0

Designed by Ceri Jones Studio, stiwdio@ceri-talybont.com
Edited by Eirian Jones and Glyn Saunders Jones
Picture research by Gill Saunders Jones
Printed by Gwasg Gomer, Llandysul, Ceredigion

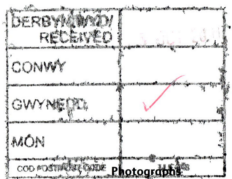

Photographs

May we thank Getty Images for their kind permission to reproduce the following photographs:
Page 6; Page 7 (top); Page 29 (top)

Contents

Wildlife at Risk

Planet Earth contains an amazing diversity of life, on land, in the air and in the oceans. However thousands of living things are now dying out each year. What's more, this is happening because of humans …

Variety of life

A **species** is a unique type of living thing, from a tiny elephant shrew to the African elephant.

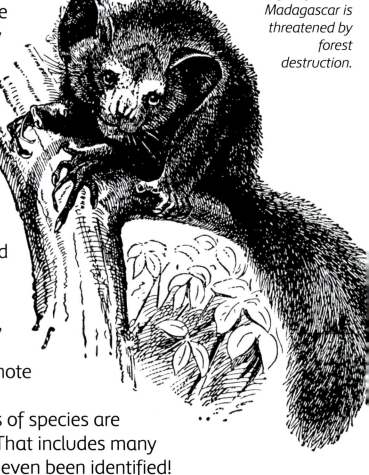

The aye-aye from Madagascar is threatened by forest destruction.

Scientists have identified 35,000 species of plants on Earth, and over a million animals. Hundreds of species are still discovered each year. Most of the discoveries are small creatures such as insects, but large mammals and birds are still found in remote places such as forests. Unfortunately, thousands of species are also dying out annually. That includes many living things that haven't even been identified!

Scottish wild cat – an endangered species.
Other endangered animals: Spix's macaw and the Yangtze dolphin

Way of the dodo

A species is said to be **extinct** when all individuals die out, so that none are left to breed. Extinctions have always happened naturally. But people are now causing a large number of extinctions, as we hunt wildlife, destroy wild places and pollute nature. In the 1600s, the dodo, a flightless bird from Mauritius, was hunted to extinction. Thousands of other species could soon go the way of the dodo if we don't take care.

The dodo

Water vole – under threat

Going, going, gone!

Species that are close to extinction are called **endangered**. Scientists believe that somewhere in the world, one species dies out every half-hour. That's 18,000 a year! On the bright side, conservationists all over the world are now working to protect wildlife. This book will explain why many kinds of wildlife are endangered, and what we can do to help.

Change and Evolution

Sea otters on the Isle of Mull, Scotland.
These otters have adapted to life on the seashore.

Life appeared on Earth about 3.8 billion years ago. Since that time scientists believe up to 500 million species may have existed. Many of these later died out, which allowed new species to develop through the process of **evolution**.

Adapt and survive

All living things are **adapted** to particular conditions in their surroundings. For example, cactus plants are able to withstand very dry conditions in deserts but would die on the seashore, while seaweeds that thrive in salt water would die in a desert. Animals that live in cold climates have thick fur, fat or feathers that provide warmth, while other species are adapted to hot climates. Species known as **generalists** survive in several different habitats, while others exist only in one tiny spot on Earth, such as on a small island.

This giant tortoise is found only on the Galapagos Islands.

Desert wildlife – the cactus and prairie hare have adapted to live with very little moisture

Natural selection

As conditions slowly change in a **habitat**, species evolve to become even better suited to their surroundings. Here's how it happens: among any generation of living things, individuals that best suit their **environment** are most likely to survive, breed and so pass on their characteristics to the next generation. Plants or animals that are less well suited may well die out before reproducing. Over time, the whole population changes to suit changing conditions. The English naturalist Charles Darwin called this process natural selection.

Sudden change

Evolution usually happens slowly, over the course of many generations. But people are now bringing fast, sweeping changes to habitats the world over. Living things must either adapt quickly, move elsewhere if they are able, or risk dying out. That's why a great many types of wildlife are currently at risk.

Yak – has adapted to live in cold climates

Camel – has adapted to live in dry climates

Living Together

Bumblebees aid plant reproduction by transferring pollen between plants. In recent years many types of bees have become rare.

The plants, animals and other living things in a habitat are called a **community**. Living things in a community rely on one another for survival. For example, animals depend on plants for food and also for oxygen to breathe. Many plants rely on animals to help them reproduce by transferring pollen or scattering seeds.

Links in a chain

The links between living things in a community are shown by food chains. Almost all food chains on Earth begin with plants, which put on leafy growth using the Sun's energy, through **photosynthesis**. Plant-eating animals, known as **herbivores**, absorb plant nutrients, which then pass to **carnivores** when the plant-eaters fall prey to predators. And so on up the food chain, to top carnivores such as big cats, bears and humans. Large numbers of small plant-eaters such as mice are needed to sustain a top predator such as a falcon or owl.

Many small prey are needed to sustain a top carnivore.
A dolphin needs to eat about 15 kg of fish a day to stay fit and healthy.

Get on the web!

Most carnivores eat a varied diet, and so are part of many food chains. These chains interlink to form a food web, which includes all species in a habitat. **Decomposers** such as beetles, fungi and bacteria are part of the web. When plants and animals die, these break down their remains. This allows **nutrients** to return to the soil or water, where they nourish more plants. So the cycle of life comes round again.

A fine balance

Life cycles and other natural processes are delicately balanced. People can easily upset the balance, for example if we wipe out an animal by hunting, or pick all of one type of plant. Unfortunately, the independence of living things means that if one link in the chain is broken, it affects the whole web.

Decomposers such as this beetle help to recycle the nutrients in dead plants and animals.

Hunting

In Africa, chimpanzees are endangered by the bushmeat trade.

Many type of wildlife are scarce because of hunting. Animals are killed for food, for their skins and other body parts. Beautiful butterflies are caught, killed and pinned to boards as souvenirs.

Meat market

Hunting has gone on since prehistoric times. But when human populations were small and hunters used spears and arrows, few animals were taken. The invention of the rifle made things easier for hunters, and a lot harder for their **quarry**. In developed countries, farming and rearing domestic animals now provides our food. But in developing countries, wild animals are still killed for meat, and as human numbers rise, so the demand for meat increases. In Africa, forest animals such as rare antelopes and monkeys are killed to provide "**bushmeat**" for locals and tourists.

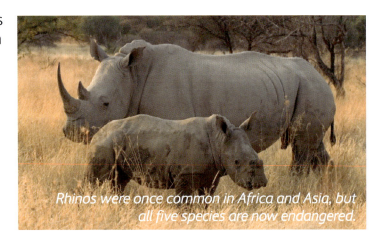

Rhinos were once common in Africa and Asia, but all five species are now endangered.

The blue morpho butterfly is endangered by collectors.

Skins, shells and body parts

Some animals are killed not for meat, but for their valuable hides, tusks and other parts. Cheetahs and leopards are killed for their beautiful spotted fur, which is made into luxury clothing. The skins of crocodiles and snakes are made into belts, boots and bags. Turtles are killed for their shells. Tiger bones are ground up and used in Chinese medicine. Elephants and rhinos are killed for their tusks and horns, which are carved into souvenirs.

Unlawful killing

So what is being done to stop the slaughter? Many countries have now passed laws to protect rare wildlife. The killing of rhinos, elephants and tigers is now banned. However horns, tusks and skins fetch high prices on the illegal market, so **poaching** goes on.

The Inuit have hunted for centuries – but they only hunt for food. Commercial fishing is the big problem.

Friend or Foe?

Powerful or dangerous animals such as tigers, sharks and poisonous snakes are often persecuted because people are frightened of them. Farmers and ranchers target animals that they believe harm crops or domestic livestock. But are these creatures really our enemies?

Seriously scary?

When predators such as foxes and jackals steal sheep and chickens, they are branded "problem" animals. Sharks, tigers and grizzly bears are labelled "man-eaters". In reality, even fierce predators such as tigers pose little threat to humankind or domestic stock. However, they do need a lot of space to hunt in. As human populations grow, so there is less and less space for large predators. Every year, sharks kill between 10 and 20 people, while people kill many thousands of sharks, so who is really the most deadly?

Keeping the balance

When top predators are removed, it affects the whole food chain. Carnivores such as lions and wolves actually help to keep nature in balance by controlling numbers of plant-eaters. In some cases, the extinction of hunters such as big cats has led to a sudden and dramatic increase in grazing animals, which have then nibbled the whole area bare.

The mako shark is hunted to make soup

Tigers are persecuted as "man-eaters". Their numbers dropped by 95 percent in the last century and three subspecies are now extinct.

The jackal is caught by trap and poison

Pest control

Plant-eating insects such as aphids are labelled as pests because they damage farmers' crops. Since the mid-1900s, farmers have used powerful **pesticides** to **eradicate** these bugs, but the poisons also harm other wildlife. In the 1950s, the **insecticide** DDT was widely sprayed on crops. It was absorbed by grain-eating mice and passed up the food chain to falcons and eagles. The predatory birds could not breed because DDT weakened their eggshells. DDT is now banned in the US and western Europe, but is still used elsewhere.

Pesticides affect birds of prey and other wildlife.

Gone Fishing

Cod, haddock and skate are now scarce

Many types of fish and other marine life are endangered by commercial fishing. Like hunting, fishing has gone on for centuries, but modern methods are so effective that some seas are almost fished out.

Big business

Fishing is a massive, high-tech industry. Modern "factory ships" use sonar and even satellites to track down shoals of fish. They put out huge nets that catch thousands of fish at once. The catch is then frozen so the fleet can stay at sea for longer, and catch more fish. Fish stocks plummet when so many fish are taken that few are left to breed. This is called overfishing. Species such as Atlantic cod and Pacific tuna, once abundant, are now scarce.

Sturgeons' eggs are sold as caviar. Even though sturgeons are a protected species, they are still hunted illegally.

Puffins rely on sand eels to feed their young.

Salmon with cream and caviar

Knock-on effects

As with food chains on land, the decline of one species affects many others. In the Atlantic, the overfishing of sand eels has harmed puffins, which feed the small, slender fish to their chicks. Dwindling fish stocks also affect mammal predators such as seals and orcas. Fishing nets and lines often catch other species besides fish, including seals and dolphins. To prevent this happening, nets can be fitted with safety hatches which allow the mammals to escape.

Sustainable fishing

Since the 1990s, over 70 million tonnes of fish and shellfish have been taken from the seas annually. These catches are not **sustainable**, and if the practice continues there will be few fish left in the seas. To preserve fish stocks, countries such as Britain now set limits called **quotas** on the numbers of fish their fishermen can catch. Nets with wider meshes are sometimes used, to allow young fish to escape and breed.

Sport and Entertainment

In developed countries we no longer hunt animals for food, but we still kill them for sport. Animals are also used to provide entertainment, but is it really fun or is it cruel?

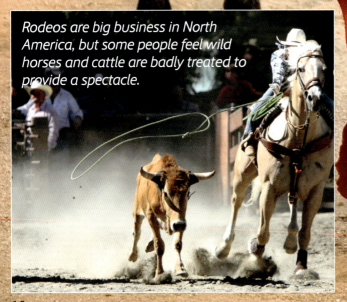

Rodeos are big business in North America, but some people feel wild horses and cattle are badly treated to provide a spectacle.

Bull-fighting is popular in Spain and some South American countries. Animal welfare groups say it is wrong to torture and kill bulls to provide entertainment.

Be a sport

In days gone by, game hunting brought about the extinction of species such as the African blue buck. In America, a bird called the passenger pigeon once existed in vast flocks, but European settlers killed them for sport, and the species died out in 1914. Hunting is still popular. Tens of thousands of deer, moose and waterfowl are shot during the open season in North America. Around the Mediterranean, 500 million birds are killed annually as they migrate between Africa and Europe.

Blood sports

Blood or field sports involve chasing and killing quarry such as deer, foxes and hares using packs of dogs. People who support blood sports justify fox-hunting on the grounds that foxes are pests, but this is not true of other quarry. They also say that hunting helps to preserve the countryside. Opponents of blood sports feel that hunting is cruel and unnecessary. Fox hunting has been banned in England and Wales since 2004, but some people want to bring it back.

Should wild animals be tamed and trained to perform tricks for our amusement?

Zoos and circuses

Many people are against blood sports, but what about zoos and circuses? Circuses with performing animals are less popular nowadays, perhaps because people believe that the animals are not always well treated. In days gone by, zoo animals were kept in cramped cages, but now many zoo enclosures are larger. Some zoos help to preserve rare species by breeding captive animals. They also offer us the chance to get close to animals we would otherwise only know from books and films.

Is fox hunting cruel or is it a good way of controlling a countryside pest?

Wildlife for Sale

Plants such as orchids are endangered because so many have been dug up from the wild.

Some types of wildlife are more valuable alive than dead. Parrots, monkeys and many species are now rare because they have been captured and sold as pets. Rather than being seen as enemies, these species are so popular that we are in danger of loving them to death!

Snatched from the wild

All sorts of animals are endangered by the pet trade. When monkeys and apes are targeted, the babies are usually taken because they are easier to handle. The parents are often killed. Caged birds are popular in many countries. Ninety species of parrots are threatened by the pet trade. Rare turtles and even poisonous snakes and spiders are also captured. Captive animals are often transported in very cramped conditions, and many don't survive the journey. The international trade in plants and animals is a multi-million pound business, which has boomed in recent years because of the internet.

Even the python is hunted!

Caged wild birds ready to be sold

Illegal trade

What is being done to protect rare species from collectors? More than 170 countries have now signed an agreement called the Convention on International Trade in Endangered Species (CITES) which bans the trade in threatened wildlife. But poachers still capture animals in secret. Ironically, the rarer the species, the higher its price on the illegal market – and the more attractive it becomes to poachers. Customs officials regularly find endangered animals being smuggled in luggage. If you want to buy a pet, ask the dealer to make sure it has been bred from animals that are already in captivity, and not taken from the wild.

African violets are endangered in the wild.

Customs officers uncover an operation to smuggle rare snakes into the country!

Alien Invaders!

Plants and animals that live naturally in a habitat are called native. All over the world, native species are threatened by new plants and animals that have been introduced by humans. The newcomers affect the whole environment as they enter the food web.

Out of control

Non-native wildlife can upset the balance of nature whether they be plant-eaters or predators. In the 1850s, European settlers released rabbits in Australia to provide food. The newcomers multiplied and nibbled the vegetation, leaving little for native plant-eaters. In the 1930s, Australian farmers introduced large, predatory toads from South America to control beetles that were eating the sugar cane crop. The poisonous toads bred rapidly and now prey on native frogs and mammals, making some species scarce.

Cane toads are now a major problem in parts of Australia.

The hedgehog has been introduced to the Hebridies and has changed wildlife there. The hedgehog eats the eggs of sea birds

Sea hyacinth smothers other water plants

Island life

Introduced species can be a particular headache on islands that contain unique animals that are unused to predators. The islands of New Zealand are home to flightless birds such as kiwis. The defenceless birds have been all but wiped out by cats, dogs, rats and ferrets that reached New Zealand as pets or as stowaways on ships. Herds of non-native sheep and cattle graze vegetation that provided food and cover for the birds.

Invading Britain

In Britain some native species are also under threat from alien invaders! The grey squirrel, which arrived from North America in the 1800s, thrives at the expense of our native red squirrel. American mink that escaped from fur farms hunt rare water voles. Even alien plants can be a nuisance! Rhododendrons, brought from Asia to ornament parks in the 1800s, have escaped into the wild where they outcompete native plants.

Vanishing Habitats

Habitats the world over are being changed or taken over by people. This is called **habitat loss**. A great many species are endangered as a result.

Too many people?
The main cause of habitat loss is growing human populations. Every year, there are more and more people on the planet. As human numbers rise, towns and cities expand, and more roads are built to connect them. Yet more land is swallowed by new estates, mines and farms. Living things are suited to particular conditions in their habitat, so they cannot just move elsewhere. And when all the wild land is taken there is nowhere to go.

Every year large numbers of badgers, foxes and owls are killed on our busy roads. Ask drivers to spare a thought for wildlife, particularly at night.

Forest homes

Forests are among the habitats that are disappearing most quickly. Woods and forests are felled for their valuable timber or to create space for new farms and towns. Tropical rainforests are particularly important because they contain great **biodiversity** (a huge range of species). Every year, over 130,000 square kilometres of tropical forest are lost, leaving animals such as parrots, gorillas and chimps without homes. It's vital that we halt this destruction, or there will be little of this amazing habitat left by 2100.

Wonderful wetlands

Wetland habitats are also vanishing as swamps and lakes are drained to create land for development. The destruction of wetlands in East Anglia led to the extinction of the Norfolk damselfly. Wetland habitats are also altered by the construction of canals and weirs for navigation, and dams to store water and generate electricity. In China, the construction of the giant Three Gorges Dam on the Yangtze River has altered the habitat of fish, amphibians and waterbirds.

Very rare monkey – Golden lion tamarin

The Norfolk damselfly died out in the 1950s thanks to the destruction of its wetland habitat.

Animal Farm

As farmlands have expanded in the last century, so there is less and less space for wildlife. On many modern farms animals are now reared in factory-like conditions. Meanwhile animals are also "farmed" in laboratories to test medicines.

Corncrake – this bird is now very rare

Shrinking grasslands

Grasslands are the main habitats that have shrunk as farmlands have expanded. Two hundred years ago the American prairies were a sea of wild grass, home to vast herds of buffalo. European settlers ploughed and fenced off the grasslands and shot buffalo for sport. The surviving animals live in reserves. In Britain, wild meadows that were home to birds like the corncrake are now "wildlife deserts", doused with chemicals to kill insect pests.

Fences prevent kangaroos from grazing on farmland.

Pigs are often reared in confined spaces

Right to roam

Livestock farming has changed a lot in the last 50 years. On most farms, domestic animals are now reared intensively. Pigs and hens are kept in cramped stalls and cages. Farmers say these conditions help to cut costs and so produce cheap meat and eggs. They say the animals benefit from protection in harsh weather. However many people feel these conditions are unnatural. Growing numbers of people are buying free-range meat and eggs, produced from pigs and chickens that roam outdoors.

So are hens

Animal testing

Science laboratories are another type of "animal farm" where mammals such as mice, rabbits, dogs and chimps are reared to test drugs and chemicals. Doctors argue that medical breakthroughs are only possible because of testing on animals. Many people would agree that experiments on animals are justified to save human lives, but not to test new soaps and shampoos. Many people now prefer to buy cosmetic products that have not been tested on animals.

Should animals be reared for laboratory tests?

Tourist Trade

Tourism became a huge industry in the 20th century. Remote beaches, forests, meadows and mountains became popular holiday destinations, but this was often bad news for local wildlife.

Coasts and coral reefs

Most people like to visit the seaside on holiday. Many wild stretches of coast have been developed for tourism, but new resorts, apartments, caravan parks and marinas can spoil wild habitats such as lagoons, coral reefs and mudflats. Coral reefs are particularly sensitive to changing conditions.

Boat anchors damage the coral. Some resorts spill sewage into the clear water, while tourists litter the beach.

Turtles come ashore to breed on remote beaches, some of which are now popular resorts.

Mountains and lowlands

In the 20th century, mountains such as the Alps and Rocky Mountains were developed for ski-tourism. The influx of visitors takes a toll on shy animals such as mountain goats, ibex and marmots. In some lowland regions, tourist developments are also eating into wild forests and grasslands.

Ski-ing is big business in many mountains, but skiers and snow-boarders can disturb shy animals such as ibex.

Treading lightly

What can be done to minimise the impact of tourism on habitats such as beaches, mountains and forests? Eco-tourism is a new, wildlife-friendly form of tourism which is catching on fast. Tourists pay to see rare species such as mountain gorillas in remote places. Some of the money goes to local people, which underlines the value of preserving the wild habitat. The rest is often used for conservation, so it's a good thing all round!

Room to breed

Wildlife such as seabirds, turtles and mountain goats need quiet places to breed. New resorts and hordes of visitors can disrupt the breeding habits of these rare animals. In national parks and reserves, breeding areas are usually roped off in the mating season, so animals can give birth and rear their young in peace.

Eco-tourists pay to see mountain gorillas in their natural habitat.

Polluted Planet

Pollution poses a serious threat to wildlife in many places. Pollution is any waste that ends up in the environment instead of being disposed of properly. Factories, power stations, vehicles and cities are all major sources of pollution.

Spreading through the chain
Pollution harms wildlife when it gets into the food chain. It is usually absorbed by small plant-eaters near the base of the chain, then passes upward via small meat-eaters to large predators. Pollution can affect the whole environment. For example, air pollution from cars, power plants and factories makes moisture in the air acidic. The moisture falls as **acid rain**, which seeps into rivers to poison salmon and frogs, which are then eaten by ospreys. Acid rain also kills plants and trees.

This osprey has caught a salmon.

Litter and waste

Pollution includes litter and junk which people drop in the country, on streets or the seashore. Rusty cans and broken bottles can injure wildlife. Plastic bags can choke predators such as dolphins when they mistake them for prey such as squid. A lot of waste is dumped deliberately, for example chemicals from industry are allowed to enter rivers. Pollution is also caused by accidents. In 2000, poisonous cyanide from a mine in eastern Europe leaked into the River Tisza in Hungary, killing almost all fish downstream.

The oil industry is responsible for a lot of pollution, including during mining, transportation and when oil is burned as fuel.

Clean it up!

It's not all doom and gloom. Many countries are now making an effort to clean up by introducing laws that reduce pollution – for example by requiring factories to filter waste gases. Many nations have signed an agreement called the Ramsar Convention which protects wetlands, and the Law of the Sea Treaty which outlaws ocean pollution.

This cormorant has got tangled in fishing line.

In 1986, highly dangerous radiation leaked from a nuclear power plant in the Ukraine following an accident. The radiation poisoned lichen on the Arctic tundra and reindeer that ate the lichen.

Changing Climate

Climate change is a new threat to wildlife worldwide. Scientists have discovered that pollution from cars, power plants and industry is trapping more of the Sun's heat in the atmosphere. This is producing **global warming** – rising temperatures on land, in the air and at sea.

Melting Arctic ice threatens polar bears.

Feeling the heat

Scientists believe that habitats all over the world are starting to feel the effects of climate change. The polar regions seem to be heating up faster than other areas. Polar ice is melting, swelling the water in the oceans. Sea levels are rising, threatening coasts and islands worldwide with their unique wildlife. The warming oceans are also harming coral, which only thrives in water of a certain temperature. On land, dry areas are getting drier, and some wetlands are drying up – bad news for frogs.

Warming ocean water can kill coral, producing an effect called bleaching.

Melting ice in the polar regions could make it harder for polar bears to find food.

Natterjack toad – climate change can affect these amphibians.

Winners and losers

As with any change, there are winners and losers. Climate change seems to be affecting the **migration** patterns of birds. In the UK, migrants such as swallows are arriving earlier and leaving later. We have gained new species such as little egrets, which were once only seen further south. Our climate could also become suitable for pests such as mosquitoes! Species that like warm conditions could benefit, but animals that are adapted to cold, such as Scottish hares and grouse, could lose out.

Bad and good news

Scientists believe that up to a third of all species could die out by 2100 because of climate change. The good news is that we can all do something to halt this global disaster in the making! Since climate change is caused by pollution from cars and conventional power stations, we can all help by using cars a bit less, using energy carefully and turning to other energy sources, such as wind and solar power.

Little egrets were once found only in southern Europe, but are now common in southern Britain.

Protecting Wildlife

Many whale species have started to recover since whaling was banned in 1985.

In the last century or so, people have spread to every part of the globe. Technology allows us to shape our environment, but we still rely on the natural world. We must learn to take better care of nature, both for wildlife and our own sake.

Planting trees helps wildlife

Natural woodland full of wildlife

Success stories

Conservation is the movement to protect wildlife and habitats. Conservation began in the late 1800s, but really took off in the 1970s, when groups such as Greenpeace campaigned against whaling, which was pushing whales close to extinction. An almost worldwide ban on whaling was agreed in 1985. In the 1980s the animal rights group Lynx campaigned against the fur trade, which

Seal cub

was endangering mammals such as wolves. Lynx changed public opinion and fur coats went out of fashion – another conservation success.

Parks and reserves

The best way to preserve many species at once is to protect whole habitats as national parks and reserves. Since the 1870s when the first parks were set up, the idea has snowballed, and there are now over 7,000 national parks worldwide. Parks and reserves have rules about not picking plants and disturbing wildlife, and building and industry are kept to a minimum. Some endangered species are now found only in protected areas.

Peregrine falcons are increasing in Britain.

Saving forest life

Biodiverse forests and woodlands worldwide are in special need of protection. Conservation groups raise money to buy huge tracts of forest in places like the Amazon. In the UK, woodlands and hedges are being replanted to help species such as dormice and owls. Check out the websites of conservation groups to find out what is happening in your area. You could organise a sponsored walk or cycle to raise money for wildlife such as gorillas and rhinos.

Back from the Brink

Tuatara in New Zealand – is under threat

People need wildlife! We depend on plants and animals for food, clothing, medicines – and vital oxygen. The world over, people are now acting to save endangered species. The first step is often to research the species' needs.

In grave danger

A species is said to be critically endangered if only a few thousand or less are left. Captive breeding programmes can help to save these species. By 1970 the Arabian oryx had all but died out in its desert habitat. Conservationists captured most of the remaining animals and bred them in zoos. In 1980 a small herd were re-released. However, for captive-bred animals to be released, suitable habitat must be found. That's why it's vital to protect wild habitats, or rare species will only survive in zoos.

Takahe in a nature reserve. This bird can only be seen on a small island near New Zealand

Drastic measures

Drastic steps are sometimes needed to protect endangered species. The survivors are sometimes moved to isolated habitats such as small offshore islands, from which all predators have been removed. In New Zealand, this measure has helped to save several flightless birds. Animals such as rhinos, that are in mortal danger of poachers, may have to be confined to reserves protected by electric fences and patrolled by armed guards.

Owl butterfly

Bring it back!

Species that have died out in one place but survive in another are called locally extinct. These are sometimes **reintroduced** from where the species is still plentiful. In the UK, the large blue butterfly has been reintroduced from Sweden. In 1993, wolves were reintroduced into Yellowstone Park, USA, where they had been hunted out in the 1920s. There's probably not enough wild space in Britain to bring wolves back, but it's a nice idea!

Wild flower meadow

Helping wildlife in the garden!

Glossary

Acid rain – Rain that is slightly acidic because of pollution from cars, factories and power stations.

Adapted – Suited to the environment.

Biodiversity – The variety of life in a particular habitat.

Bleaching – When coral dies and turns pale.

Bushmeat – Wild animals that are killed for food, usually in Africa.

Carnivore – An animal that eats meat.

Community – All the living things found in a particular habitat.

Conservation – Work done to protect the natural world.

Decomposer – A living thing that breaks down dead matter.

Endangered – Of species that are at risk of dying out.

Environment – The surroundings in which people or wildlife live.

Eradicate – To wipe out.

Evolution – When a species changes over time as it adapts to its surroundings.

Extinct – When a species dies out completely.

Generalist – Of a species that lives in a number of different habitats.

Global warming – Rising temperatures worldwide, caused by an increase of gases in the atmosphere that trap the Sun's heat.

Habitat – A place where particular plants and animals live, such as a desert or rainforest.

Habitat loss – When a wild habitat is taken over or changed by people.

Herbivore – An animal that eats plants.

Insecticide – A poison used for killing insects.

Introduce – When people bring a new species into a habitat.

Migration – A seasonal journey undertaken by animals to breed, find food or escape harsh conditions.

Nutrients – Chemicals that living things need to grow.

Pesticide – A chemical sprayed on crops to protect them from weeds, insects or fungi.

Photosynthesis – The process by which plants live and grow using sunlight energy and minerals and water from the soil.

Poaching – When hunters kill or capture animals or other living things that are protected by law.

Pollution – Any harmful substance that damages the environment.

Quarry – An animal that is targeted by hunters.

Quota – A limit on the number of certain types of fish that can be caught.

Reintroduce – When people return a species to the wild in an area where it has died out.

Species – A particular type of living thing, such as the African violet or black rhino.

Sustainable – When resources are harvested without damaging the environment.